A Place for Everyone

Tana Reiff

A PACEMAKER LifeTimes™ BOOK

A Place for Everyone

Tana Reiff
AR B.L.: 2.8
Points: 0.5   UG

LifeTimes™ Titles

Editorial Director: Robert G. Bander
Managing Designer: Kauthar Hawkins
Cover, text design, and illustrations: Wayne Snyder
and Teresa Snyder

All characters herein are fictional. Any
resemblance to real persons is purely coincidental.

ISBN 0-8224-4318-X
Printed in the United States of America

7 8 9 10 11 12   06 05 04 03 02

Globe
Fearon

Pearson Learning Group

1-800-321-3106
www.pearsonlearning.com

Contents

CHAPTER 1

Dot sat
at her sewing machine.
She had a dress to make
for Mrs. Lopez.
There was a hem to sew
for Mrs. Fulton.

Dot liked to sew.
She made
all her own clothes.
During the day
she had a job
in a factory.
At night she worked
on her sewing.
Most of the sewing
was little jobs
for women
she knew.
They liked
Dot's work

because she sewed
fast and well.
Sewing for herself
and others
kept her
very busy
when she was at home.

Dot was
about 40 years old.
She was not married.
She and her mother
lived together
in a little house.
They were happy.

But Dot wanted
more in life.
She wanted to sew
for a living.
Not in a factory,
but on her own.
She wished she could have
her own business.
She wanted to be
her own boss.

She knew she would have
enough work to do.
Sometimes people
had to wait for weeks
because Dot was so busy.

But something was standing
in Dot's way.
She couldn't read very well.
And she knew
she would have to read well
to run her own business.
She knew
she had a problem.
But she had never done anything
about it.

There was something else, too.
Dot wanted to be
the first person
in her family
to get a high school diploma.

One night
Dot and her mother
saw an ad on TV.

The ad told about
a school.
An adult could study
at this school
for a high school diploma.

Dot's mother asked,
"Why don't you
go to that school?"

"Who, me?
I don't know,"
said Dot.
"They might laugh
at the way
I read."

"I don't think so,"
said Dot's mother.
"Why don't you go
and see what it's like?"

"I'll think about it,"
said Dot.

Thinking It Over

1. Do you think a person
   ever stops learning?
   Why or why not?

2. What more do you want
   in life?
   Do you think you'll ever
   get it?

3. How important is reading
   in your life?

4. Why is it hard
   for some people
   to go back to school?

CHAPTER 2

Since Dot
worked during the day,
she went
to the school
at night.

"My name is Dot.
Will you tell me
about the school?"

"Hello, Dot.
I'm Chuck.
I'll take you
around the school
and tell you about it.
At this school
you work as fast
or as slow
as you want.
The teachers
help every student.

You don't
have to keep up
with anyone.
You do
as much as you can.
You go
as far as you can go."

Chuck seemed
like a nice young man.
He spoke again.

"This is
the reading room.
It's where
our students work
on their reading,
of course.
This is where I teach."

"I don't read very well,"
said Dot.

"That's OK, Dot,"
said Chuck.
"We will help you."

Then Dot asked,
"Will I
be able to get
my high school diploma?"

"Maybe,"
Chuck said.
"If you work very hard,
you might.
If you can learn
enough to pass
the high school diploma test.
I can't say for sure
right now.
But why don't you
give it a try?"
It really seemed as if
Chuck wanted Dot
to come to the school.

Dot still wasn't sure
what she should do.
"Are there any kids
at this school?
I don't want kids
to see how I read."

"No kids
at this school,"
said Chuck.
"And we are all friends here.
Don't be afraid."

"Well, all right,"
said Dot.
"When can I start?"

Thinking It Over

1. How do you like to learn—
   in a group
   or by yourself?

2. Do you think
   adults should go to school
   with kids?
   Why or why not?

CHAPTER 3

Dot's first night
at school
was Monday.
Chuck was her teacher.
He gave her a book.
They worked on that
for a little while.
Then they worked
on a newspaper.

"Tell me more about
the high school diploma test,"
said Dot.
"What is it all about?"

Chuck smiled.
"It's called the G.E.D. test.
But it's
a long way off, Dot.
Let's just work
on your reading.

Don't worry
about the G.E.D. now, OK?"

"OK," said Dot.
"But what does
G.E.D. mean?"

"It means
you are tested on your
General Educational Development,"
said Chuck.

Dot asked,
"Will you tell me
when I'm ready
to take the G.E.D.?"

"Yes," said Chuck.
"But why don't you
take a break now, Dot?"

All the students
took a break.
They went out
to have a cold drink
or something to eat.

They talked
to each other.

Dot liked
to meet new people.
She started to talk
to a woman named Maria.

She asked her,
"Are you going
for your G.E.D.?"

"Yes," said Maria.
"I want to take the test
in two months.
I want to get
a better job."

"Me too,"
said Dot.
"How long
have you been working
for your G.E.D.?"

"Oh, not too long,"
said Maria.

"I've been coming here
four nights a week
for five months."

"Really?
That's a long time,"
said Dot.
"You must really
want that diploma."

"I do,"
said Maria.
"It means a lot to me."

Thinking It Over

1. Is there something you want
   that you will work hard
   to get?

2. What do you like to read?
   What don't you
   like to read?
   Why?

CHAPTER 4

"Mother,"
called Dot.
"Are you home yet?"

"I'm in here,"
her mother said.
"In the kitchen.
I just got home.
I stayed
to see the movie tonight."

Dot's mother
sold tickets
at a movie house.

"It was
a great movie!
It was about people
going up into space.
Tonight was
the first night,

so I stayed
to see the movie.
I saw it twice!
How was school?"

"Oh, it was all right,"
said Dot.
"My teacher
is very nice."

"You don't look
very happy,"
said her mother.

"Well, I was talking
to a woman
named Maria.
She is going to take
her G.E.D. test soon.
She has been going to school
for five months.
I will have to work
much longer—
maybe even a year—
before I am ready.
That's a long time.

I don't know
if I can make it."

"Maybe you should
stop thinking about it
so much.
Worrying about it
will not help.
Just go to school
and work,"
said Dot's mother.
"You can't
do more than that now!"

"You forget, Mother.
I am doing
more than that now,"
said Dot.
"I'm sewing.
It seems to be
a good way
to earn money.
Not a lot
of money.
But enough.
I've started

a business
of my own—
right at home.
And I like it."

"You're doing
a lot of
nice work.
That's for sure,
dear,"
said Dot's mother.
"But don't try
to do everything
at once."

"Maybe you're right,"
said Dot.

"Well, I'm going to bed.
I don't feel well.
Maybe I had
too much movie!"
Dot's mother
said good night
and went to bed.

Thinking It Over

1. What do you think
    about giving up?
    Can it be good
    as well as not so good?
    Why?

2. What does it mean when
    someone says to take "one
    step at a time"?

CHAPTER 5

One night
when Dot
was sewing at home,
the doorbell rang.
It was Mrs. Lopez.
She looked happy.
She told Dot
how much she liked
the long yellow dress
Dot had made for her
last month.

"I wore it
to my company party,"
Mrs. Lopez said.
"And it was
a smash hit."

"I'm so glad
it looked good,"
Dot said.

"I want you
to know
that I think
your sewing is
beautiful,"
Mrs. Lopez went on.
"I don't have
a sewing order
for you tonight.
But I hope
you will promise me
one thing.
My daughter
is being married
next summer.
I want you
to make dresses
for the whole wedding party—
the wedding dress,
the bridesmaids' dresses,
my dress,
maybe even
the dress for the groom's mother.
Will you do it?
Can you
promise me that, Dot?"

Dot's eyes opened wide.
"Of course,"
she said.
"Of course I can, Mrs. Lopez."

Thinking It Over

1.   What is the nicest surprise
     you have ever had?

2.   Do you believe
     the saying
     "Nothing succeeds
     like success"?

CHAPTER 6

Her sewing work
seemed to be going better
for Dot
than her work at school.
But she could tell
that she was
reading better.
She went to school
four nights a week.

One night
Maria wasn't there.

Dot asked Chuck,
"Where is Maria?"

"She called me today,"
Chuck said.
"Her little boy
fell out of a tree.
He broke his arm.

Maria has to
take care of him."

"That's too bad,"
said Dot.
She knew Maria wanted
to take the G.E.D. test
in three weeks.
Now she might not
be able to.

It didn't seem fair.
Some students could
come to school
every night,
but they didn't.
Maria wanted to come
every night,
and she couldn't.
That's life,
thought Dot.

Then she thought
of her mother.
Her mother had not been well.
If she got really sick,

Dot would have to
take care of her.
Dot would not
be able to come
to school,
just like Maria.

She opened her book
and began to read.
The book
had been too hard
when she started school.
Now she could read it.

When she got home,
the house was dark.
She called,
"Are you home, Mother?"
Her mother did not
call back to her.
Dot thought her mother
must have stayed
to watch a movie.

But she asked again,
"Are you here, Mother?"

She looked
in the kitchen.
Her mother
wasn't there.
She looked
in the living room.
No one was there.
She looked
in her mother's bedroom.

Her mother
was on the floor,
face down.

Dot cried,
"Oh, Mother!"

Thinking It Over

1. Do you ever
    get angry at someone
    who has a chance to do
    something and doesn't do it?
    Why do you think
    such people
    don't take the chance?

2. Have you ever felt
    your own reading
    getting better?

3. What do you do
    when something is hard
    for you?

CHAPTER 7

Dot's mother
was still alive.

Dot ran to the telephone
and called the doctor.
In ten minutes,
a car came
to take Dot's mother
to the hospital.
Dot went along.

She asked the doctor,
"Will she be all right?"
She didn't know
what she would do
without her mother.

"I think she'll live,"
said the doctor.
"But she will have to stay
home in bed

for a long time.
Only that way
will she get well."

Well, well, thought Dot.
This is just what
I was thinking about.
My mother is sick,
and I must
take care of her.
But what will she do
when I'm at work?
And what about school?
And what about my sewing?

Dot didn't
have to worry
for long.
The next day
she went to work.
Her boss called
all the workers
into one place.

"I have bad news,"
he said.

"We must close down
the factory.
We are not making any money.
We must lay off
all of you.
I am very sorry."

Dot was sad
to leave her job.
But now
she could stay home
and take care of her mother.
Her mother would get out
of the hospital soon.
It would work out well.
Dot knew
she could make enough money
to live on
from sewing full time.
And she was glad
her mother had
a health plan.
It would pay
most of the hospital bills.

Thinking It Over

1. Why was Dot sure
    she could make
    enough money?

2. When someone gets laid off
    from work,
    how might he or she
    make ends meet?

3. How would you feel about life
    if you were Dot?

CHAPTER 8

Dot went to school
that night.
She told Chuck
what was going on.

"It will be very hard for you
to take care of your mother,"
said Chuck.
"And since you must sew
at night,
I see why
you can no longer come to school.
We will miss you, Dot.
But maybe
you can come back
when your mother
gets well."

"Chuck," said Dot,
"I do want
to help my mother.

But I also want to get
my G.E.D.
someday."

"I know,"
said Chuck.
"And even though
you won't be in school,
you can still
work toward it.
You can work on
your reading
at home.
Reading is
the key
to the test."

"Tell me, Chuck,"
said Dot.
"Will I ever get
my G.E.D.?
Will I
ever read well enough?"

"I don't know, Dot,"
said Chuck.

"But there are
other things in life.
The G.E.D.
isn't everything.
Right now
your mother needs you.
And you'll
take good care of her.
You're good
at lots of things."
Chuck was trying
to make Dot
feel better.

"I know
I'm not good
at school,"
Dot said.
"Even *wanting* to be good
doesn't help.
But there *do*
seem to be
things I'm good at
without even trying hard.
Like my
sewing business."

"You're a
really strong person, Dot,"
said Chuck.
"And you have
real talent.
Most important,
you have taken
the steps
to make that talent
work in your life."

"Thanks, Chuck,
I needed that,"
said Dot.
"Good-bye.
I hope I'll see you
again sometime."

As she walked
out the door,
Chuck called to her.
"Wait a minute, Dot,"
he said.
"Why don't you
take some books
with you?"

With her arms
full of books,
Dot walked out
of the school.
She didn't know
if she would ever be back.
And she didn't know
if she would ever
get her G.E.D.

Thinking It Over

1. Did you ever
   want something so much that
   you couldn't stop thinking
   about it?
   What was it?

2. Do you think a person
   shouldn't try to do things
   that are hard?
   Why or why not?

3. Do you think
   everyone needs
   a high school diploma?

CHAPTER 9

Soon Dot's mother
came home
from the hospital.
She was still very sick.
She needed
a lot of help
from Dot.

Dot cooked
and cleaned.
She fed her mother
and tried to make her happy.

When her mother
was resting,
Dot sewed
a lot.
She made a coat
for Mrs. Perez.
Then she telephoned
Mrs. Perez

to tell her
that the coat
was ready
to be picked up.
Dot called
three other women too.
She let them know
she had started
a sewing business.
One of the women
she called
was Mrs. Farr,
a friend of
her mother.
Mrs. Farr had some work
for Dot to do.

Then one day,
Dot's mother asked,
"Why don't you
read to me?"

"Oh, I can't do that,"
said Dot.
"I'm not good enough
to read to you."

"Please try,"
said her mother.
"I won't laugh at you.
I want to hear
what's in the newspaper."

"OK," said Dot.
"What do you want me
to read?"

"The part that tells
who died today,"
said her mother.

Dot asked,
"Why do you want
to hear that?"

Her mother said,
"I just want
to make sure
my name is not there!"

Dot read
as much as she could.
It was fun.

Her mother helped her
with the hard words.
Then Dot read
the comics.
Then she read
some want ads.
Then she tried to read
a news story or two.

Every day
Dot read to her mother.
Every day
she got better at it.
She read the books
from Chuck.
Her mother liked them too.

After she had read
all of Chuck's books,
Dot wanted more.
She went out
to a store.
She wanted to buy
her own books.
She looked at some.
They had such nice covers.

But they were too hard
for Dot to read.

A clerk asked her,
"May I help you?"

Dot was afraid
to tell the clerk
her problem.
Then she said,
"Do you have
any books
that are easy to read?"

"Why, yes,"
said the clerk.
"We have children's books."

"No," said Dot.
"I want something
for myself."

The clerk showed her
some comic books.
They were famous books
made into comic books.

They had
lots of pictures.
And they were cheap.

Dot took
10 of them
home with her.

When she had time,
Dot sat in a big chair
and read to herself.
It made her
feel good.
She could feel her reading
getting better
all the time.

Thinking It Over

1. Is there anyone you help who helps you, too?

2. What books do you like the best?

3. What parts of the newspaper do you read the most? Why?

4. Do you ever
   read books
   at home
   for fun or learning?

CHAPTER 10

Dot's mother
got better and better.
Soon she could walk around
a little bit.
But she still was not
well enough
to stay by herself.

Now Dot had more time
to build
her sewing business.
She started to catch up
on a pile of sewing.

One day as she started to sew,
someone came to the door.
Dot went to see
who was there.

"Hello, Dot!"
It was Mrs. Farr.

"Dot, your mother tells me
you have some time now.
Can you fix
some more things for me?"

Dot looked
at what Mrs. Farr had.
"Yes, I think
I can do that."

"Fine," said Mrs. Farr.
"Can I pick them up
on Monday?"

As Dot was working
on Mrs. Farr's things,
the telephone rang.
It was Mrs. Perez.
She wanted to know
if Dot could
make her
a long dress.
Dot thought
for a minute
about her
back orders.

Then she told
Mrs. Perez
she would sew the dress.

A little while later,
someone else
rang the doorbell.
Dot went to the door.

"Hello, Dot."
It was Mrs. Rose.
Dot did not know her.
"Mrs. Farr says
you sew so well.
Can you fix
these things?"

"Oh, my,"
said Dot.
She took the things
from Mrs. Rose
and looked at them.
There were
two pairs of slacks
that needed fixing.
And two dresses

that needed to be
made shorter.
Dot told Mrs. Rose
her things would be ready
on Tuesday.

Dot thought again
about wanting to sew
for a living.
I'm going to do it,
she thought.
If I keep on getting
lots of orders,
it will work for me.
But how can I start
a real business?

She went
to talk to Chuck.

"How can I start
my own business
in the right way,
Chuck?
There must be
some things

I'm not doing
that I should
know about,"
she said.

"First you must fill out
a lot of papers,"
said Chuck.
"Then you must keep
careful records.
You must keep track
of all the money.
You must write down
what you spend
and what you make.
You can get the papers
at City Hall.
I'll help you
fill them out."

Things were
starting to happen.
Soon Dot
would have
a real business.

Thinking It Over

1. What have you ever
   done or bought
   because you heard about it
   from a friend?

2. If you make up your mind
   to do something,
   do you stick to it?
   Why or why not?

3. If you tell someone
   something will be done,
   do you do it on time?
   Why or why not?

CHAPTER 11

Things were working out
very well.
Dot had
lots of sewing to do.
She was making plans
for her business.
And her mother
was getting well.
Dot still read to her
every day.

One day
Dot's old boss called.
"Dot, we are starting
a new factory.
We want you
to come work for us.
Will you do it?"

Dot just didn't know
what to say.

"I'll call you back,"
she said.

Dot really had
something to think about.

The factory job
would mean sure money
every week.
Still, the sewing business
would be more fun.
But she could not be sure
about the money.
The money wouldn't come in
every two weeks
the way it did
at the factory.
But so far,
the money from her sewing
had been good.
She had
lots of orders.
And almost every week
she got new ones.
And what about
her mother?

Who would
take care of her?
It was time
to talk to her mother.

"I'm much better,"
said Dot's mother.
"I think I can
take care of myself now.
If you want to go back to work,
it's OK with me.
What do you
want to do?"

"I don't know.
But I like to sew.
I like it better
than working in a factory."
Dot was really
up in the air.

"Well," said her mother.
"It's up to you.
Do what you want to do.
I know you will do
the right thing."

Thinking It Over

1. Would you rather
    work for a lot of money
    at a job you didn't like
    or make less money
    at a job you liked?

2. What things
    can you do
    to help you
    keep a job?

CHAPTER 12

Dot made up her mind.
She didn't
take the factory job.
She decided to stay
with her sewing.
She set up
her business.
She handled
all kinds of sewing.
She did
small jobs,
like sewing hems.
And she did
big jobs,
like making slacks and coats
for women
who wanted
the very best in clothes.
She also
started to sew
men's clothes.

She made money
doing all this.
Not as much
as she would have made
at the factory.
But enough for her and her mother
to live on.

Keeping track
of the money
was hard
for Dot.
She spent
too much time
doing it.
She didn't know how
to do the taxes.
The papers were
hard to read.
And if they were not done right,
she could get
into trouble.

So Dot went back to school.
When she saw Chuck,
she asked about Maria.

"Where is Maria?
How is she?"

"Maria took her G.E.D.
last month,"
said Chuck.
"She passed!
Now she has
her high school diploma."

"Oh, that's so nice,"
said Dot.
"Maria needed that G.E.D.
But you know what?
I've decided
I don't need it
as much as I thought
I did."

"What made you
change your mind?"

"Well, my reading
is much better,"
said Dot.
"I needed that

more than I need
my G.E.D.
I can see now
that the G.E.D.
is a long way off
for me.
But right now
I must learn more
about numbers."

"You might still
get your G.E.D. someday,"
said Chuck.
"Who knows?"

"That would be nice,"
said Dot.
"I'll work hard.
I'll learn to read
as well as I can.
I'll learn more
about numbers.
But I must take
one thing at a time.
I see that now.
I've learned a lot

about myself
these last few weeks.
I took good care
of my mother.
I have
a good sewing business now.
And I can read
so much better.
I see now
that I'm good
at lots of things.
Now my life
is in order."

"It's great
to hear you
say that, Dot,"
said Chuck.
"I knew all along
that you were good
at a lot of things.
You just had to
find out for yourself.
It's nice to have you
back at school.
Let's get to work."

Thinking It Over

1. If you want to know
   more about something,
   what do you do?

2. Do you think
   that every person
   is good at something?
   Why or why not?

3. List 10 things
   you are good at.

4. Have you ever heard
   this saying:
   "A place for everything
   and everything in its place"?
   Do you think
   there is a place
   for *everyone,* too?